AF448731

Puppy Training

A Beginner's Guide to Potty Training, Obedience Training and Behavior Training

Catalina Morris

© Text Copyright 2022 by Catalina Morris - All rights reserved.

The information herein is offered for informational purposes solely, and is universal as so. The presentation of the information is without contract or any type of guarantee assurance.

The trademarks that are used are without any consent, and the publication of the trademark is without permission or backing by the trademark owner. All trademarks and brands within this book are for clarifying purposes only and are owned by the owners themselves, not affiliated with this document.

Table of Contents

CHAPTER FIVE

CHAPTER SIX

CHAPTER SEVEN

CHAPTER EIGHT

Introduction

Once you have found the perfect puppy to join your family, you need to make sure your new friend is adequately trained. Training your puppy will help him understand what is expected and gain confidence. Proper training will also strengthen the bond between you and your puppy and make it possible for you to include your puppy in your daily activities more often. A well-trained puppy is a happy, well-balanced puppy, and of course, that's what you want for your new best friend.

There are different theories about how to train a puppy. Some people believe in firmness and strict commands. Others tell you that providing rewards for good behavior and taking away rewards for bad behavior is essential. The best course of action will depend on your dog's personality.

This book will make puppy training a whole lot easier for you. It features proven methods and step-by-step instructions for training your puppy and introducing him to your home, your visitors, and the general public. Chapter 1 helps you understand your puppy and his personality, Chapter 2 provides you with helpful puppy training tips, and Chapter 3 explains crate training. Potty training is one of the most critical tasks to teach your puppy when he comes home, and Chapter 4 covers it in depth. In addition, Chapter 5 introduces the best way to teach him obedience commands, Chapter 6 introduces clicker training, and Chapter 7 shows you how to walk your puppy. Finally, Chapter 8 contains key tips on how to stop destructive behaviors.

While it may seem daunting to teach a new puppy everything he needs to know, the truth is that puppies are usually very eager to please their new families. When training your new puppy, you're bound to make mistakes, and your pet will too. With patience and consistency, your puppy will learn what he is supposed to do, and you will be well on your way to building an incredibly satisfying, lifelong friendship that will be more rewarding than you ever thought possible.

CHAPTER ONE

Understanding Your Puppy

If you want to train your puppy properly, you need to understand what is causing him to act the way he does. You have to understand his psychology, and you'll be surprised to learn how much he resembles a child. It's your job to read your puppy's behavior and adjust the training accordingly.

Dog Psychology

Think of your dog as an infant that will grow quickly. He is born with certain instincts, but this won't teach him what he needs to know to become a beloved member of your household. The puppy's mother will use imprints on his memory to teach him, and you'll have to learn to do the same. You'll need to teach him to smell certain things to tell if the smell is good or bad, and you'll need to use imitation as well. It's important for him to imitate you. For example, if you bark, then he will bark.

If you always turn electronics, such as the TV, off at night, then your puppy will learn that these lights being turned off mean that it's bedtime. Your puppy will learn these routines through your habits, where consistency comes in handy. Associate learning is another process that you'll need to teach your dog. Associate learning is tying a motivational reason or a reward to the training. He is motivated by instinct, which makes him want love, shelter, food, and water.

A puppy has needs and desires that you're supposed to meet as an owner. You have to teach your puppy appropriate actions and ignore any inappropriate behavior. If you give your puppy attention for his negative behavior, he will start to associate that behavior with the ability to get your attention. Keep in mind that your puppy has emotions. He can be fearful, bored, worried, happy, sad, and even depressed. It's up to you to be able to interpret these feelings.

Dogs are followers. This is why training a puppy with an already trained adult dog is so much easier. This way, he has something to model his behavior from.

Puppy's Personality

A puppy will start to develop his personality at about seven weeks. His full personality can usually be seen at ten to twelve weeks. If you want to choose a puppy based on his personality, it's important to wait at least seven weeks. You should visit your puppy before finalizing your choice at ten to twelve weeks to check on his personality again.

Keep in mind that the environment he is kept in can affect his personality. Your puppy may act differently where he was born versus your home. Genetics will also factor into your puppy's personality. Different breeds have different traits, so you must read up on dog breeds before picking one.

CHAPTER TWO

Puppy Training Tips

Puppies are naturally playful, curious, and active. Those traits will be fun most of the time, but to keep your friend safe and protected, you want to help him establish boundaries. The best tip to start with is to think about your puppy like you would a human child. Treat him as if he were an infant or a toddler. Here are some puppy training tips that you can use to teach your puppy everything he needs to know to start the journey of becoming your best friend.

Puppy Proofing Your Home

One of the first things you will need to do with a new puppy is puppy-proof your home. Your little dog is probably not housebroken yet, and you don't want to clean up messes throughout your home. Keeping the puppy within your range of sight for the first few weeks is essential.

Indoors

 • Tiny objects that can be easily swallowed up, such as coins or rubber bands, should be kept out of reach.

 • Never leave food lying around. Alcohol, chocolate, coffee, onions, and sugar can cause severe problems to your puppy's digestive system. Tobacco, smoking patches, and nicotine gum can be fatal if ingested. Be aware that food scraps, such as chicken bones, coffee grounds, or uncooked meats, can be a health hazard to your puppy.

• Puppies love to chew on electrical and cable cords, which can cause burns or electric shock. You can buy cord concealers or protective cable wrap to keep your electrical cords and your puppy safe.

• Never leave CDs or DVDs lying around. A puppy can chew them into sharp shards, which will do some serious damage.

• Everyday cleaning supplies should be kept out of the puppy's reach or behind childproof locks. Also, keep in mind that toxic vapors can get into the puppy's eyes and lungs while you are cleaning. Your puppy should be kept in another room.

• All medications and vitamins should be kept out of the puppy's reach. Never keep pills on the counter, table, or dresser. Your curious puppy can easily chew through a plastic container and happily do so if given a chance.

• Bathtubs and sinks filled with water are a potential drowning hazard. Also, keep the lid on your toilet.

• Space heaters, fireplaces, or candles should never be left on when your puppy is alone in a room, even for a minute.

• Put any sentimental or precious items out of the puppy's reach. Even if they're not toxic, you want to ensure your puppy doesn't decide some beloved old photograph is a fun chew toy.

• some puppies mistake cat feces for food! If you have a cat, keep its litter box separated from the puppy by using a baby gate.

• Keep your puppy where there's flooring (tile, wood, etc.), so it will be easy for you to clean.

Outdoors

• If you have a yard, your puppy needs to be in a fenced-in area or an outdoor kennel to keep him from straying and investigating the neighborhood.

• A swimming pool is a real problem. You could put a cover over the pool until your puppy is old enough.

• Take care of the lawn regularly. Ticks can be hazardous for puppies.

• If there are toxic plants in your yard, get rid of them, as your puppy can mistake them for a snack.

• If your yard has been treated with pesticides, keep your puppy away from it.

• Be sure to block any access to a shed or garage that contains insecticide, gasoline, paint, oil, or fertilizer. Your puppy will like the taste of rat poison or antifreeze, which can be fatal.

• Clean up after your puppy and make sure he doesn't eat his waste.

• Pick a place in your yard to make it the puppy's bathroom. This will instill good habits and save you from cleaning feces from all over the yard.

Choosing a Collar

A collar is a functional accessory that your dog will wear around his neck. The collar can attach to a leash or a harness when it's time to go for a walk, and it can also be used to hold any dog tags or documentation that you received when you registered your puppy.

When gathering your supplies, buy items that can grow with your puppy. Collars should be adjustable and checked frequently for a proper fit. Puppies grow quickly, and you do not want the collar to be too tight or uncomfortable. When fitting your puppy's collar, be sure that you can fit two fingers between the collar and his neck. This measurement will help ensure the collar is snug enough to keep your puppy secure but won't be tight and uncomfortable. If your puppy starts to scratch at his collar, distract him with a toy, treat, or with verbal distractions to take his mind off it. When you're shopping for collars, make sure the collar you select has a sturdy metal ring to attach the leash to when you begin to leash train and walk your puppy.

Habits start in puppyhood, so you want to make sure you're reinforcing good behavior and punishing bad behavior. It's never too early to start. If you've got a bit of a barker on your hands, you can find a collar that discourages barking. Choose a chain collar for stubborn pups who are tempted to take off or refuse to move when they need to.

Choosing a Leash

The leash accompanies the collar, especially if you don't have an outdoor space where your puppy can run free. It might seem like walking on a leash should be second nature to your puppy, but it's a learned behavior.

Look for a leash that is secure and fits nicely on the collar or the harness you're using. When selecting the first leash to use for your puppy, pick one that is lightweight. A heavy leash may add pressure to the puppy's neck and make leash training more difficult than it needs to be. Give the puppy enough leash space to roam independently, but not so much leash that the dog can run into traffic or get into trouble. Retractable leashes are often a good option because you can decide how much freedom you want to give your little buddy.

Treats and Rewards

Everyone, including puppies, loves treats. You can use these as a reward for good behavior. Dog treats come in all flavors, sizes, and specialties. Soft, meaty treats are very enticing to most puppies, and having a ready supply on hand will help your puppy quickly learn what behaviors are wanted and rewarded. Puppies usually love treats with cheese, peanut butter, or meat flavor. Select small treats instead of big ones that require a lot of chewing. The trick with training is to use quick, positive reinforcement and small, bite-sized treats as a perfect reward for your puppy.

Provide a treat anytime the puppy goes to the bathroom outside or sits and rolls over when commanded. Don't give your dog treats for no reason, or this will confuse the situation, and he won't realize he's being rewarded.

Your rewards should also vary. If you always give him a treat following a voice command, he will associate the command with food. He'll refuse the command if he doesn't want or need food. Instead, if your rewards include giving him a treat, soothing him, playing with him, or petting him, he knows that he will get some type of reward when following the command. This way, a puppy will learn to always listen to his commands.

Communicating Your Intentions Clearly

There's nothing wrong with explicitly telling your puppy "no," only that it often fails to offer enough information. Instead, you can tell him what you want. Dogs don't usually generalize well, so if the dog jumps on someone in excitement and you say "no," he may jump higher or change direction. A better alternative would be to instruct him to sit. Telling him what you want helps avoid confusion.

One of the biggest mistakes when using voice commands is to use too many words. Your dog can associate words, but it takes some time. You'll want a word that is to the point. Finish learning one command before moving on to another. If you move on to other commands too quickly, then your dog may get confused.

Be Consistent

You have to be consistent if you want your puppy to be consistent. You can't work for an hour on a sit command and then just not take up his training again for a week or two. You have to work on the same command until he gets it right.

Establish routines with your puppy, such as regular feeding times, walk and play times, and bathroom breaks. Stick with your routines, and this will help speed up the process. It's not just about training commands, either. A routine for your puppy will help him get up when you do, play when you feel up to it, and eat when you are able to feed him. This way, you aren't rearranging your schedule to take care of your puppy. Instead, you'll be teaching him to work on your schedule so that he works with you.

If you don't want your puppy to jump on people when they come through the front door, you need to reinforce that expectation every time. Allowing the pup to jump all over your sister but not your neighbor will cause confusion. Use the "sit" or "stay" or "heel" command to get your puppy's attention, and do it every time.

Use Repetition

Repetition is key in dog training. For example, ask your dog to sit and give him a treat for the first two times. For the third time, try a different type of reward, such as petting and praise. This will teach him that he gets rewarded in different ways by listening to your commands, and this type of repetition can be extremely useful in training your puppy.

Be Patient

Don't allow yourself to get frustrated or impatient during the training process—either with yourself or with your new puppy. It will take some time to accomplish all the goals you have set for your new pal and for you to get the hang of your puppy's personality, likes, and the techniques and rewards that work best for your puppy.

Give your puppy time to understand new commands. He most likely won't learn it the first couple of times when you teach him. Repeat old commands in new training sessions so that he doesn't forget them. The attention span of a dog is pretty short, so keep your sessions frequent but short in duration; otherwise, your pup will become bored.

Never get impatient with your puppy and never call him to you if you are going to punish him—all that will do is teach him that coming to you is not a good thing. Keep your voice firm but gentle, and never let any frustration creep into it.

Training Yourself

When you introduce a new dog into your household and your life, you're not just training the puppy. You're training yourself as well. Your life will have to change, and you need to be prepared for it and willing to adapt. Sleeping in until noon on the weekends is no longer an option when you have a puppy that needs to be walked and fed. Taking off for a spontaneous vacation sounds like fun, but first, you'll have to make arrangements for the pup. Working with the dog to be calm and quiet when friends and family visit takes a lot of energy and a willingness to hang in there for the long term.

You are working on forming a lifelong bond. Be patient and consistent with the process, and it will work. All the puppy training tips in the world won't work if you have a short fuse or lack interest in making your puppy comfortable and well-behaved. Puppies are adorable, but they're also a lot of work. Before you take the plunge into new puppy ownership, make sure you're willing to invest the time, emotional energy, and resources. For specific puppy training tips, you can call on experts in the field. Pet stores, veterinarians, and fellow dog owners can all help you and your puppy become good roommates and family members.

CHAPTER THREE

Crate Training for Puppy

It might seem cruel—the idea of confining a dog to a metal crate. However, crates make puppies feel safe and secure as they mimic the dog's natural den habitat. Crate training your puppy is an excellent idea, especially if you want your dog to sleep in the crate at night or you plan to be out of the house for most of the day. This keeps your puppy from destroying your house while you cannot supervise him. While there might be some whimpering and resistance the first time you confine your pup to a crate, the training will work quickly.

Choosing a Crate

Crates come in many different sizes, and you can find crates that are metal, plastic, and even fabric. When shopping for a crate, look for crates just large enough for your puppy to stand and turn around in. If your puppy will soon grow too large for a crate, look for larger crates that include a crate divider. This way, you can use the crate divider to block off half the crate until your puppy grows large enough to fill the crate space, and you avoid the expense of buying multiple crates.

Creating a Den

Prepare the crate by making sure it's clean and in a quiet, private area of the house. Dogs like a view, so if you have a nice window next to which you can place the crate—even better. Some people like to put a toy or a blanket in the crate for a puppy. This is a great idea, but if your dog is prone to chewing things to shreds, you might want to wait until you have that behavior modified. Puppies need a den that is clear of debris. Many people also find that placing an article of their clothing or an old towel inside the crate is a good idea; the dog will be comforted by your scent.

Crate Training Steps

You have to introduce the crate slowly and make sure you do it casually. You can't just bring your puppy home and then throw him in a crate. You certainly can't just lock him inside of it. You have to make the crate seem like it's a casual piece of furniture in your home.

First, introduce your dog to the crate. Some puppies will immediately be curious and might even start to explore the crate, walking in and out freely. If your puppy isn't that curious or relaxed, sit next to the crate and encourage your dog to come to you. Keep your tone and your voice happy and positive. Keep the crate door open but not so loose that it can swing shut or scare the puppy.

Drop some small treats into the crate to encourage your puppy to go in there alone. If the dog doesn't want to go all the way in, don't force him. Give him time to understand that it's safe and chase those treats. Some people have had success by feeding their puppies meals in the crate. Place a small bowl of food and water in there and see if your pup is willing to enter. This is especially useful if you'll be leaving the house for work every day. It's important your puppy eats and drinks without defecating in the same place because he will be there all day. This will help him to try to control his bladder.

Once your puppy is comfortable going in and out of the crate (which could take a few days), begin closing the door of the crate. Sit next to the crate for 10 or 20 minutes the first time you do this. Once your puppy relaxes, get up and leave the room. You might hear barking or whining, and that's okay. Come back into the room after about 10 minutes and sit next to the crate again. Then, let the puppy out. Keep repeating this until you can leave the room without your puppy barking.

You don't want to teach your puppy that barking or whining will get him out of the crate. The whining should stop before you open the door. If you open the door immediately, he'll start to associate whining as the way to get you to open the door. The behavior will only increase. Although, you need to be careful not to create stress in your puppy. It would be best to gradually increase the time your puppy stays in the crate.

When you and your puppy get to the point that entering the crate is not a struggle and you can be in another room for half an hour without any barking or begging, you can probably leave the house and safely keep your puppy in the crate. Try not to be gone too long. Puppies don't have the bladder strength of older dogs, and they will need to go outside every few hours.

For Nighttime

You'll want to make this a part of your puppy's daily routine. If you want a dog to sleep in a crate, you need to get him started with that schedule from the first day. Your puppy will whine at first, but you should ignore him and maybe keep the lights on low. Your puppy will start to associate quietness and darkness with bedtime, so he'll know to stop whining.

You'll have to be patient until you get your puppy to that point. However, if your dog doesn't stop whining in a week, you'll want to find a room where there isn't anything to destroy and no stimulation. Close the door, leave the crate open inside of it, and let your puppy associate this with his routine. He'll likely sleep in the crate at night. Many puppies just want the offer of freedom that a closed crate does not allow for.

One thing you should never do is use the crate as a punishment. Don't put your puppy in there as retaliation for misbehaving, barking, or biting. Crate training requires a feeling of comfort and security for your pup.

All dogs are different. You might have a puppy who loves the crate, or you might have a puppy who needs constant treats as bribes to get into the crate. If your puppy associates the crate with a safe place, you'll eventually be able to tell when he is feeling stressed, insecure, or sick by watching how often he goes into the crate.

CHAPTER FOUR

Potty Training

For many people, potty training their puppy is the most daunting part of bringing a new puppy into the family. Potty training a puppy can be time-consuming and messy. However, it's essential for your dog's growth and development, as well as your peace of mind.

Puppies younger than twelve to sixteen weeks old simply do not have enough control over their bladders to be potty trained. Until your puppy is twelve weeks old, keep a supply of disposable or washable puppy pads your puppy can use.

These pads usually have a scent that attracts the puppy to eliminate. If your dog doesn't go on the pad, even when he is trained, instead of thinking you have a bad dog, you'll want to consider that he doesn't like the smell of the pad. It may smell amazing to you, but it may irritate his overly sensitive nose.

How to Use Puppy Pads

1. Clear the Room: You'll want to mark out a clear space to train him. You need to clear the room so that your dog isn't confused by anything. A playpen will sometimes work if you have a small breed but never use a closet. You don't want your dog to feel like you don't love him and are punishing him. A storage room will help, and so will a spare bedroom.

2. Plastic: Put some plastic on the floor to protect your flooring.

3. Newspaper: Next, you will cover the plastic with newspaper because it is easier to clean.

4. Puppy Pads: You'll then place two or three puppy pads in the room.

5. Sleeping Space: You'll need to have a puppy bed or a crate so that your puppy has a designated sleeping space in the same room.

6. Food & Water: Your new puppy will be spending a lot of time here, so make sure that you have a dedicated area for food and water that your dog can get used to as well.

7. Pay Attention: You have to pay attention to signs of when your dog needs to relieve himself. Twirling in circles, whining, scratching, and sniffing the floor are often indications the puppy needs to potty. When he starts to show these signs, you have to carry him to the puppy pad. He doesn't know to go to it yet, so this is your responsibility as his owner.

8. Be Persistent: When your puppy tries to walk away or starts to sniff another area, pick him up and place him back on the pad. Make sure to do this gently and calmly so that you're correcting the behavior but not punishing him.

9. Provide Treats: Once your dog goes on the pad, you need to immediately reward him with a treat.

10. Keep repeating: You'll need to keep repeating all of this so that he understands he should potty on the pads.

The age of your puppy determines just how frequently he has to use the bathroom. Make sure you clean up any space that's been soiled, so he won't attempt to go there again. You need to remove the odor, which is why you put the plastic down to make your job easier. You can then start to provide a clean pad every time for your puppy.

For Outside Bathrooms

If you don't want to have him going in the house, you'll want to train him to go outside. Hold off on outside potty training until your puppy is at least twelve weeks old. You have to choose the rules on where you want him to do his business, so you must train him to go inside or outside early on. Outside takes a little more dedication, and here are the steps to train your puppy.

1. Every Hour: You need to start by taking your puppy out every hour, making sure to go with him. You will need to take your puppy out immediately after he wakes up, 15 minutes after he eats or drinks, at least once an hour while he is awake before you put him in his crate, and immediately after you take him out of the crate. To help prevent accidents, be sure you keep your puppy on a regular feeding schedule and remove the food once he has finished eating, but always allow him access to water. Your puppy's digestive system is quick and efficient, and taking him out 15 minutes after he eats will help get him used to going potty outside.

Puppies cannot be expected to hold their bladders all night, so you will also need to set the alarm during the night to take him outside. Expecting your puppy to hold his bladder throughout the night is not only unrealistic, it is a sure-fire way to ensure he soils his crate or gets a bladder infection trying to hold it far longer than he is capable of or should be expected to. It is also important to watch for bathroom "tells" puppies often display. If you see or hear these things, take him outside immediately

2. Call Him: You can call him by name or put a leash on him to have him follow you. Be consistent on which you use.

3. Pick an Area: You can pick a spot and train him like you would with a puppy pad. It is important that you take your puppy to the same spot every time to use the bathroom. Your dog will be able to sniff the area and tell where he went to the bathroom before. Be patient with your puppy, do not try to force him, yell at him, or rush him to use the potty. Simply stand in the designated spot and use upbeat, positive verbal encouragements to "go potty" and allow your puppy time to sniff out the perfect spot and relieve himself. Once your puppy does his business, be sure to reward him with positive praise, a treat, a lot of snuggles, pets, or kisses. Make it a rewarding, happy experience, so your dog feels good when he sees you get the leash and say the words "go potty." Most puppies want to please their masters, and letting your puppy know he is good and did the right thing will help your puppy's potty training progress at a faster rate.

If He Doesn't Listen

If your dog doesn't listen, you need to provide more training. Pay attention to what he likes. Does he like praise more than treats? Are you making sure to vary it? You should have started with treats and progressed to praise. Also, you could be trying to rush your puppy. If you rush him, he won't go to the right area because he feels the need to hurry. Puppies can pick up on your impatience, so try to calm down.

How to Handle Accidents

Accidents are going to happen. Sometimes when a young puppy gets excited, he can accidentally use the bathroom without meaning. Just accept accidents as part of the process and do not overreact to them. Your puppy is not being willful, disobedient, or resistant. Do not punish him by spanking him, rubbing his nose in it, or yelling at him. If you notice your pup begins to pee or poop in the house, clap your hands or make a loud noise. You want to startle the puppy and get its attention, but you don't want to scare him. Calmly say "no" and take him to his spot outside.

When an accident does occur in the house, simply clean it up and move on. You cannot apply a correction after the fact—the puppy will have no idea what is going on, why he is being told "no," or what he was supposed to do. Unlike us, puppies live in the moment, and once it has passed, they do not have a recollection of the accident, so trying to discipline a puppy for a past action will only make him scared and make it difficult for him to trust you. Never, ever strike your puppy when you find accidents or for any other reason. Hitting your puppy will only crush his spirit and break the bond you are trying to build; it will not correct his behavior or make the process faster.

Be patient and consistent with your potty training routine and be gentle, kind, and loving with your puppy. You'd never yell at, punish, or berate a baby for accidents, so don't do it to your puppy. Follow these potty training tips, and in just a few weeks, your puppy will be potty trained, and you can feel good about a job well done.

CHAPTER FIVE

Obedience Training

There are many different theories about how to train a puppy. Some people believe in firmness and strict commands that come with consequences. Other schools of thought will tell you that providing rewards for good behavior and taking away rewards with bad behavior is the best way to train a puppy. The best course of action depends on your dog and the animal's specific personality. Some puppies will be interested in pleasing you, and others will not really care what you think. The best way to approach obedience training with your puppy is to use consistent practice. Remember that puppies are young and active, so keep your training sessions short and make sure they are not hungry or tired.

Teaching to Heel

Teaching your puppy how to heel is important, especially when there are other dogs around or people that your dog might want to jump on without invitation. When you command your dog to heel, the dog will sit by your side quietly until released. This is difficult for puppies to learn, especially since they are so energetic and curious by nature.

The key to this part of puppy training is, of course, treats. Start by standing with your puppy on a leash and keep a few treats in the hand that isn't holding the leash. The puppy needs to understand the command, so tell your dog to heel. Once he sits still next to you for about five seconds, give the dog a treat. Then, take five steps forward and allow your dog to follow. Say the word "heel" and wait for your puppy to sit down next to you. Reward with a treat. Continue doing this, so your puppy understands. The dog will associate your movements and words with the expected behaviors.

Once this is successfully completed in the same location, introduce other people and distractions. You might feel like you're starting the process all over again, but that's only because your puppy will notice those other people or bouncing balls or moving cars. Repeat the process with the treats until your dog is obedient and able to heel on command.

Teaching to Sit

Teaching your puppy to sit is not complicated, and the dog will understand what you want when you reward with treats and physically show the animal what you expect. When you teach a puppy to sit, you are not only teaching him that you are in charge, but that if he wants any reward, he will have to sit on the ground and behave. This also keeps dogs from jumping up on people or taking food from people's hands in the house.

The first thing is to get a treat for your puppy. Make sure you have a quiet place to train your dog, free from distractions. Stand in front of your puppy and hold your hand above his head with a treat in it. He will look up at it. Use your other hand to gently push down on his hindquarters until he's in a sitting position. At the same time, while still holding the treat, say "sit" in a calm but firm voice. Once he can hold the position, give the puppy the treat.

Repeat this process about ten more times. If the puppy sits for you when the treat is held above his head, you are ready to move on to the next step. If not, continue repeating this step until the dog sits on command.

The next step is to hold your hand out without the treat and tell your puppy to sit. If the dog sits, reward him with three treats, then take a break.

The next day, start with the empty-handed motion while repeating the word "sit" and providing the puppy with one treat. When you are sure the puppy fully grasps the sit command, you can choose to stop saying sit and use only the hand motion to get the dog to sit, providing treats each time he obeys.

Make sure your puppy understands the command completely. However, as we all know, we cannot continue to feed the dog treats every time we tell him to do something. Therefore, you need to begin cutting back on the number of treats you give the puppy. One way to do this is to give your puppy a treat every other time he obeys the command, then every third time, and so on, until you no longer give the dog a treat for sitting.

Be sure only to teach your puppy one command at a time. Once the dog understands that command, continue to practice for five minutes each day. As you practice, increase the distractions the puppy is exposed to while you tell him to sit, which will prepare him for the distractions he will face outside of your home, or when he becomes excited and needs to be brought under control.

You can also practice telling your puppy to sit in the middle of playtime. Run around with your puppy, play, stop suddenly, and tell him to sit.

If your puppy temporarily loses the training you've mastered, simply start again. You might notice your puppy jumps on people when they come into your house or runs after children in the neighborhood. Give the command to sit, and if the dog does not listen, go back to the basics with the treat and the physical lowering of your dog into the sitting position.

Teaching to Lie Down

The next command is the lie-down command. This is a good command for your puppy to learn so you can keep him in one spot and help calm him. This is also an excellent way to handle barking.

Once again, find a quiet place to teach your puppy the command. Begin by telling your puppy to sit, show the dog the treat in your hand, bring it down to the floor, and say "down." It is a good idea to close the treat in your fist when you bring it down to the floor, so the puppy will know that it is there but that he's not allowed to take it from you. As the puppy lowers his body down to the floor in the lying position, give him the treat.

Bring your puppy back to the sitting position and repeat the process about ten times. After the dog has gotten used to getting a treat for lying down, you can stop bringing your hand to the floor, but instead, simply tell the puppy to lie down. If the dog does as he is told, give him three treats. If not, go back to the first step until he understands that the command "lie down" is followed by the treat, and try again.

After he has followed the command without you having to lower your hand to the floor, take a break. The next day, practice ten times, having the dog lie down without bringing your hand to the floor.

After your puppy has mastered this step, repeat the same process, but this time without a treat in your hand. Again, after the puppy has mastered this, begin reducing the number of treats the dog receives until the dog no longer receives treats for the behavior.

Teaching to Stay

Teaching a puppy to stay is difficult because it's counterintuitive to a puppy who wants to explore and jump and sniff and bark. The stay command is important for your puppy to learn because it will teach him self-control and help ensure the dog does not bolt out the front door when you are trying to leave.

Teach your dog the stay command after he has mastered the sit and lie-down commands. Find a quiet place for you to train the dog. Begin by commanding your puppy to sit. After the dog is in the sit position, tell the dog to "stay," wait two seconds, and give the dog a treat. Increase the amount of time you make the dog wait for the treat until the dog can wait for ten seconds, each time, telling the dog to stay.

Each time you say "stay," put up your hand, flat, with the palm facing the dog. This will become your hand command once your dog learns how to stay. If the dog gets up from the sitting position, say "no," have the dog sit again, and start the process over.

When the dog can stay in the sitting position for ten seconds without getting up, continue the process, but this time take one step away from the dog. Repeat the word "stay." Take two more steps, and again repeat the word "stay." Finally, step out of the dog's sight.

Continue to work with the puppy until you can stay out of the dog's sight for two minutes without him moving. After the puppy has mastered this skill, start again, but this time begin with the lie-down position and have the dog learn to stay from there.

Teaching to Come

Puppies always want to come when they're called. They want to know what you're up to, and they're going to be eager to be close to you and be a part of whatever you're doing. However, it can be difficult to get your puppy to come if the dog is preoccupied with something else. Maybe the puppy is digging in the backyard or stalking a squirrel or utterly obsessed with the scent on some random car's tires. The trick is to teach the dog that coming to you is the best decision that could ever be made. When you call your puppy's name, and your little buddy comes running over, shower that dog with praise and love and treats. With that kind of affection and positive reinforcement, your puppy will never want to miss the opportunity to come to you when called.

For training purposes, call your puppy from one room to another. When your puppy is in the living room, stand in the kitchen, and call the dog by name. When your puppy comes running, get excited, pet him and provide a treat. When the puppy understands that coming when called means only positive things, he will obey immediately.

Teaching "No"

You teach your puppy the "no" command only when he exhibits bad behavior. Training your puppy to respond to the "no" word can save you a lot of trouble. The steps used to teach a dog the "no" command are similar to the other basic commands. First of all, whenever you find your puppy doing something unwanted, such as jumping on the sofa or barking, immediately clap your hands and say, "no," at the same time. Clapping your hands will distract your dog from what he is doing and most likely stop his actions. Be sure to say the word "no" in a firm, loud voice, but only say it once because you're training the dog to listen the first time. If the puppy obeys, give him a treat and a lot of praise, and redirect the dog to something else. For example, if he is chewing on a piece of clothing, give him a toy. Again, consistency and patience are required. You won't be able to train your new puppy overnight. However, with time and structure, obedience training can be conquered.

CHAPTER SIX

Clicker Training

For many puppies, a clicker is a great way to train them. Small and inexpensive, clickers work by capturing your dog's attention with an audible sound. This method helps stop your dog from being dependent on the treats and still listen to you. You won't have to call or yell at your puppy, and he can hear the clicker at a long-range.

Simply press the clicker's button when your puppy does what you want him to do and follow the click with a positive reward, such as a small treat or an enthusiastic, encouraging pat, a scratch behind the ears, and a "good boy/girl!" verbal reinforcement.

Step by Step

Here is a step-by-step on how to train your dog using a clicker. Make sure you get a clicker that works well to get started.

1. Use a Command: You have to start with a goal in mind. What behavior do you want to target first? One of the best ones to target is "sit." Raise your hand with a treat visible in it and tell your puppy to sit.

2. Treat: Make sure that you give the treat once he is in the correct position. You don't want to have too long of a delay, or this will hurt the association process.

3. Repeat: Do it all over again, and make sure that you use the same movement and tone.

4. Vary Reward: Do it a few more times, and then you'll need to vary the reward you're giving him. Sometimes just pet him, sometimes say "good boy/girl!" and sometimes use the treat.

5. Clicker: Once the puppy has already made the association, that's when the clicker comes in. Repeat the process of asking him to sit, then press the clicker's button, and follow the click with a positive reward, such as a small treat or an encouraging pat. He doesn't know what the new noise is yet.

6. Repeat: This time, you're going to tell your dog to sit, holding the clicker and treat over his head. Remember to click it as you lift it. Give him a treat. Keep repeating.

7. Clicker: Use just the clicker, and if your dog sits, give him a treat. You don't have to use words now.

Make sure that you never train your dog in a way where the clicker just gets his attention. You need to assign it to a certain command. Keep in mind that some dogs will learn slower than others, and you can't expect your puppy to learn to respond to the clicker in just a day or two. When you teach your dog another command with the clicker, you need to vary the clicking. One click may be "sit," but two rapid clicks will need to be something like "lie down." However, if you want to add another such as "stay," you can use three rapid clicks or two slow clicks. If you have a hard time with your puppy not listening, try giving him a break. Just like kids, he sometimes needs to go out for recess, and school can't be every single day.

CHAPTER SEVEN

Going for Walks

Your puppy needs exercise and fresh air to help him stay calm, grow healthy, and get the stimulation he needs to stave off boredom and the destructive behaviors that often accompany boredom. While playing with your puppy is fun and provides some exercise, walking your puppy is the best way to help him expend pent-up energy and calm his mind. Once your puppy is leash trained, walking him is an enjoyable way for the two of you to bond and provides you with time to clear your mind and get some exercise, too.

The Normal Puppy

An untrained puppy isn't aware of the dangers around him. He will strain against his leash, and he'll hate that he can't get free. He'll buck, jump, and do anything he can to get out of his harness or collar. He'll also want to stop and smell everything he can. A puppy gets a lot of information from his sense of smell, and he can tell if something is good or bad, if another animal has been around, or even if it's just interesting to him. He will often forget he's on a leash at all, and he may wrap around you if you aren't careful. He may try to run ahead and pull you with him if he can. The following leash training tips will have you proudly walking a well-behaved, happy pup sooner than you ever thought possible.

Introduce the Collar

There are dozens of different collar and leash styles to choose from, and the best one for you will depend on your dog. Small dogs do well in a harness, so they can't slip out of their collars. That works well for puppies of all breeds.

When you first introduce the collar to your pup, be sure it fits properly. There should be enough room for you to fit two fingers between the collar and your pup's neck. Make putting the collar on fun by using an upbeat but calm voice and reward your pup with a treat once the collar is fastened. Some puppies will try to push the collar off or scratch at it; after all, it is a new sensation. If your pup does this, distract him with a toy, a treat, or scratching behind his ears. Anytime you see your puppy messing with his collar, apply a positive distraction, and soon your puppy won't even notice he's wearing a collar.

Introduce the Leash

Once your puppy is used to the collar, it's time to introduce him to the leash. Select a lightweight leash so there is no unnecessary pulling that may make your puppy leery of the leash. Clip the leash onto the collar and call your puppy to you. Some puppies will have a major reaction to the leash and thrash around wildly trying to get it off. This is normal, so simply drop the leash and allow your puppy to pull it behind him as he wriggles, squirms, and hops. Do not let your puppy out of your sight since the leash can become caught up on something and hurt him. Continue to put the leash on for short periods, dropping down to one knee and calling your puppy to you with a reward when he comes. Once he reaches you, pick up the leash and walk him short distances around the house. Repeat this a couple of times a day until your puppy is accustomed to the leash. Make the process fun by verbally praising your puppy and offering treats. If he tries to bite the leash, remember to tell him "no." Never let your puppy treat his leash like a toy.

After your puppy understands the sit and stay commands, you can teach him the "walk" command. You can do this with or without the clicker. Walk to your puppy, and say "walk" while you start walking. You should give him a treat if he walks in the same direction as you. You then ask him to sit and then stay, and remember to praise good behavior. You'll need to repeat this process until he starts to associate the word "walk" with the movement you're making.

Never pull or tug harshly on the leash, fight your puppy on the leash, or yell at your puppy, as those negative behaviors will only confuse the puppy and set your training back. Be patient with your pup and keep a consistent routine of attaching the leash and letting your pup get used to it slowly and at his own pace.

His First Walk

By now, your puppy is used to walking short distances inside the house on a leash, and it's time to take the fun outside. The outside world offers a lot of fun and distraction, so even though your pup knows how to be led on the leash, he may act differently outside.

Go to the door, and when your puppy follows, you'll need to tell him to sit and stay. Then you're going to put the harness or collar and leash on, finally opening the door. If the puppy reaches the end of his leash, tell him to sit and stay. If he shows improper behavior due to excitement, just ignore it. Give him a treat when he follows the commands.

If he pulls, stop, stand completely still, and do not move until he comes back to you. If he is becoming too much to handle, always try the sit and stay command instead of pulling or shortening the leash he's on. Let your dog smell things, use the bathroom, have fun, and walk around the space with you. Be patient. Start with short walks at first, and soon you and your pup can increase the time and distance.

Just make sure you stay in the leadership role and repeat the process with different rewards. He'll start to eventually associate his collar or harness and the leash with walking with you, which will make him excited.

You can start to add new commands as you test new boundaries with your puppy. For example, if you put the leash on the left, you can teach him to turn left. If you have it on the right, he can learn to turn right. When it's just straight above him, then your puppy will know to keep walking straight. If you want to teach your dog to walk without a leash eventually, you can start by teaching him hand signals. When he starts listening to how to walk, he is ready for trails, dog parks, and other new places.

If He Sees Another Dog

Your dog is bound to get excited with his new adventures. If your puppy sees another dog, he will likely want to rush up to them. He might want to do this if he sees another person too, which means he could forget the commands you taught him. You'll have to remind him that he listens to you by tightening or shortening the leash a little. This will pull your puppy right towards you, which will limit his ability to pull away or jump.

Tell your puppy to sit and repeat the command, and then tell him to stay. Reward him if he exhibits proper behavior. It can take several tries to get him to calm down, but this is essential to training a puppy correctly. This is why it's important to have treats with you when you take your puppy on walks. Most of the time, telling him he's good and petting him is enough, but sometimes a treat is needed or just wanted. Food is one of your most powerful motivators, but make sure that you change where you keep the treats on you. You don't want your puppy just to start listening because he sees you going for a treat.

The Length of Walks

You may be wondering how long your puppy should be on his walk, and this is based on different factors. Keep in mind how warm it is, how much stamina he has, and how long you want to go on a walk. If the temperature is too hot or too cold, you won't want to take your dog on a long walk. If it's too hot, make sure that you keep a lot of water on you. A dehydrated puppy can get sick.

Puppies have different stamina based on their breeds. If they have fat bodies or shot legs, then they're not going to be able to walk as long or as far. If you have a bigger breed that's known for its endurance, then an hour's walk may be right up their alley. You should read up on your dog breed to know how long your walks should be. Distance is up to you since you're the leader, but don't forget to keep his stamina and the weather in mind.

Crossing Roads

You don't want your puppy to be so excited that he crosses the road without you and gets hurt by accident. This is one reason you taught him to sit and stay. It's important to ask him to sit and stay at crossroads before giving him the walk command. This is important even if your puppy is on a leash. Puppies do sometimes get off leashes, and it will decrease the chance of him getting hurt by a car if he knows to sit and wait at a crossing. This process is slow, especially with how excited he is when he's out, so make sure you're willing to put in the time and effort.

If He Refuses to Come Inside

One issue you may face is that your puppy refuses to come inside after the walk. Some people think this is very cute when the dog is just a puppy, and often they will pick the puppy up and carry him into the house, but this is the wrong thing to do. You see, at some point, depending on the breed of dog, the puppy may become too heavy for you to carry inside. Another mistake many people make is that they drag him inside by pulling on the collar.

You can use treats to entice your puppy to keep walking and coax the dog into the house. Eventually, you can stop giving the dog treats for going inside after a walk. Understand that the reason why your puppy doesn't want to come in after a walk is that there's so much for him to see outside—like things to sniff and other dogs for him to meet—but going back inside is boring.

While it can be frustrating and require more patience on your part, you have to make the transition back inside the house less boring for your puppy. One good way to do this is to create playtime inside. Rather than leave him to his own devices, grab your puppy's favorite toy and play with him for a few minutes after the two of you finish your walk.

Finally, you might want to consider extending your walks. Often, dogs are not ready to come back inside because they have not gotten enough exercise and are still full of energy. When you extend the walk, you allow the puppy to burn up more energy, which means he will be more likely to come into the house without an issue.

CHAPTER EIGHT

Behavior Training for Puppies

If you're a puppy, you feel like the entire world has been created for you to enjoy. You want to play and run and bark and jump and bite. For puppies to become well-behaved household pets, they need to be trained in what acceptable behavior is and what isn't. While it might be fun to watch your puppy acting cute—it's not fun to listen to barking, pick up scraps of what was once your favorite pair of slippers or repair the once-landscaped backyard that has been dug to pieces. Behavior training for your puppy is necessary for your peace of mind and your little dog's protection.

Chewing

Chewing is a behavior that comes naturally to dogs; however, it can also cause a lot of damage. Puppies usually begin chewing because they explore the world with their mouths. However, they need to understand what is acceptable to chew on and what is off-limits. If they chew on the wrong thing, they can cost their owners a lot of money and may even cost them their lives.

It is important to understand that a puppy will chew more when teething because this is a painful process, and chewing gives him some relief from the pain. If a puppy chews on the wrong items, it is most likely to happen while he is teething. If chewing is not controlled during this time, it can become a tough habit to break later on.

When teaching your puppy not to chew on inappropriate items, you should first make sure no underlying medical conditions are causing the puppy to chew. There are specific dietary issues, parasites, and intestinal problems that can cause this.

The next step is to puppy-proof your house. Look around your home to make sure your puppy does not have access to anything that might put his life in danger. Ensure all household chemicals are put up and away from the puppy and that all power cords are covered so the puppy cannot get to them. Remove any objects the puppy might find interesting, such as socks or shoes.

It is best to restrict the puppy to a small area, such as the living room. This can be done using baby gates on the doorways inside the living room. It will also make it easier on you to keep the puppy from getting into things he shouldn't.

Give your puppy items that are okay for him to chew on. Each dog will have a different preference for what he likes, so it is a good idea to provide him with a few toys of different textures. Be careful with rawhide and beef bones because the puppy can chew on these until a small piece breaks off that could fit in the puppy's mouth and cause him to choke.

Make sure the toys you provide for your puppy are of the appropriate size. The dog must be able to pick the toy up easily and carry it around. However, it needs to be big enough that he will not swallow it. If you purchase a toy that has any type of hole in it, make sure the hole is not big enough for the dog to get his jaw stuck in it.

Do not give your puppy toys that look like items you don't want him to chew on. For example, many owners purchase a toy that looks like a shoe while telling the dog not to chew on shoes. You should also avoid giving the dog an old shoe to chew on if you hope to teach him not to chew on new shoes.

By providing the puppy with items that he is allowed to chew and keeping inappropriate items out of his reach, you will make a lot of progress to ensure that he does not wrap his teeth around anything inappropriate.

If you find the dog chewing on an item he should not be chewing on, it is important to take the item away from him and state in a loud voice, "no." Put the item away so that he understands he is not supposed to chew on it. After taking the item away from the puppy, you redirect his attention by providing him with one of the toys he can chew on.

If you find the puppy has a hard time understanding which items he should not chew on, spray the items with Bitter Apple as a deterrent. If an item tastes bitter, the dog is less likely to chew on it.

You should also make sure your dog is getting enough exercise. A bored dog is likely to search for items he can chew. Be sure to spend time each day taking your puppy for walks, playing with him, and just spending time together. Not only will this make the bond between the two of you stronger, but it will also ensure the puppy does not destroy items that are important to you.

Barking

The next behavior to get under control is barking. Dogs bark for a variety of reasons. Most owners eventually learn what each of their dog's barks means. For example, a dog may bark in a specific way if he needs to go outside, he will bark differently if he needs food or water, and he will bark in another way if he wants to play. Dogs also bark to warn other animals to stay away, sound an alarm alerting their owner of danger, or just because they want to bark.

Of course, you don't want to stop your puppy from every kind of barking. It is best to make sure the dog can warn you of danger or scare off anyone or anything that could harm you, but stop him from barking over you when you are talking or sleeping at night.

Your aim should be to stop the puppy from barking when there is no reason for him to bark. Many people make the huge mistake of paying attention to the dog when he barks or tell him to be quiet in a loud voice, which makes the dog think you are proud of his barking, and to him, you are joining in with the barking as you 'bark' loud commands for him to be quiet.

To get your puppy's barking under control, you must first get to know the dog so you can begin to understand what situations might cause him to bark. When you understand why he barks, you will be able to take control of the situation and show the dog you are a confident leader for him to follow. Once you get the dog, you have to build a strong bond with him. He has to be able to trust you and know you will take control of any situation.

There are several different ways for you to control unnecessary barking. Some people recommend holding the dog's mouth gently closed when he is barking. This is not the best way to teach your dog not to bark. Other people think you should keep the dog's mouth busy with a toy; however, you must be careful to use this approach because the dog may think he is being rewarded for the barking behavior.

It is important for you to teach your puppy the "quiet" command. Consistently say "quiet" in a firm and calm voice when you want him to stop barking. After he stops barking, reward him with praise and a treat. After he has mastered the command, begin giving treats less and less often until you no longer provide treats for this behavior.

Some barking can be ignored. Expect some barking when you first crate train a puppy because he's getting used to his surroundings and will try to do whatever he can to get you to take him out of the crate. The barking will cease with time and can be ignored for the most part.

The barking you should not ignore is when the dog barks for the sake of barking. Barking in and of itself can be rewarding for the dog, as he is having fun, and if you allow him to continue, he will think it is okay.

When you take the dog outside, be sure not to allow him to bark at those passing by or run the fence line, chasing cars as they pass by. When you show the dog you are the one in control of his behavior, he will accept that you decide when and where he can bark.

Biting

There are many reasons why dogs become aggressive and bite. The dog may feel overexcited or threatened. Much dog aggression comes from a lack of confidence and positive training. It is important that you socialize your dog with different people, dogs, children, and environments. Socialization will boost his confidence and reduce his fear in new environments.

Teaching a dog not to bite is vital. Most people do not enjoy playing with a dog known for mouthing, chewing, or biting on hands, clothing, or other body parts. You need to get this type of behavior under control early on because as the puppy gets older, it is much less likely he will be sensitive to your reaction when he bites. It is likely that an adult dog who bites or chews on people was not taught to be gentle when he was a puppy.

Mouthing is a natural behavior for dogs because they explore the world with their mouths. On the other hand, biting is a reaction to either fear or frustration. It is important for you to be able to tell the difference between playful mouthing and aggressive biting. You see, most people enjoy wrestling with their dogs, and they have no problem placing their hands in the dogs' mouths, which helps to build trust between the people and their dogs. Owners need to know that their dogs will not viciously bite them. When a dog is play mouthing, the dog's body will be relaxed, his tail will wag, and although his face may be wrinkled, it is obvious from his behavior that he is not being aggressive.

An angry or frightened dog, on the other hand, will have a stiff body, his muscles will be tense, and his tail will be straight. Most of the time, the dog will mouth a person before the bite as a warning, but this is not always the case.

If you want to teach your puppy not to bite or mouth your body parts or clothing, spend some time playing with him. Allow the puppy to mouth your hand as you play, but as soon as he does, let out a yelp as if the puppy has seriously hurt you, and allow your hand to go limp, startling your dog. This should immediately stop the puppy from mouthing your hand. Praise the dog for stopping. Often you will find that the dog will lick your hand. Resume play, and repeat the process if the dog mouths you again. Play with your pup for about 15 minutes. Continue to do this every day until the dog no longer mouths you.

Mouthing is another reason it is important to provide your dog with various chew toys of different textures. When the puppy has the toys, he is less likely to bite during playtime.

Digging

Some dogs will turn their owner's yards upside down, making the owner feel like they are doing it all on purpose. However, dogs dig for various reasons, none of them being to get revenge on their owners. Dogs dig because they are bored, seeking attention, hunting prey, entertaining themselves, or seeking protection, to name a few reasons.

The first thing to do if you want to stop your puppy from digging is to find out why the dog is digging in the first place. If the dog is left alone and outside for long periods with no one to keep him company, he may begin digging. In this case, ensure that you go outside and play with him. It is also a good idea to ensure that he has plenty of toys to play with. Make sure you walk the dog at least twice each day to guarantee he is getting enough exercise and stimulation.

If your puppy is digging for prey, it will most likely be near the roots of trees. You can take steps to fence the animal out or use humane ways to catch the animal and move it to a safer place. However, you should never use poison of any type because the poison can also hurt or kill your puppy.

Dogs will dig large holes to lay in if they are left outside in hot weather or shield themselves from the cold, wind, or rain. This means the dog is searching for comfort, as well as protection.

To prevent this, make sure your puppy has adequate shelter while outside. You can also bring the dog inside more often to protect him from extreme weather.

Make sure that the dog has a full bowl of water and that there is no way for the bowl to flip over. If the dog prefers to lay in a hole in the ground, make sure he has an area in the yard where he can dig.

A dog may also dig as a way to get attention. Often this happens when the dog does not get enough time with or attention from the owner. The only way to stop this behavior is to provide the dog with the love and attention he deserves.

Dogs also dig as a way to escape. This can occur if the dog tries to get something outside of the pen or tries to get away from something. The first thing you need to do is figure out if he is trying to get to something outside of the pen and remove the item from his view. The next thing you need to do is make sure the pen is inviting and appealing to your dog.

You also need to think about your home. If the environment is stressful to the puppy, he may try to dig under the fence to get away. If there is a lot of yelling, arguing, and stress in the home, the dog will feel it, and he won't be comfortable there. Make sure you do your best to provide your puppy with a safe and loving environment so he will not want to run away.

You can bury chicken wire under the fencing of the dog's pen, but make sure that any sharp edges are turned outwards and away from the puppy. You can also place large rocks partially buried at the bottom of the fence. However, you should not punish the puppy after he has been digging because this will only cause him to feel more anxiety and make him want to get away.

Behavior training for puppies might seem overwhelming, but if you follow these tips, you'll have a well-behaved dog in no time.

Conclusion

If you want to raise your puppy into a good dog who knows what is expected, you need to train him. Always be in the right mindset, and be willing to pick up training at another time if things start to get out of control. Each puppy learns at a different pace, so you have to work with your puppy. Start your training right away, and don't give up until you have the behaviors you want from your puppy.

Finally, I want to thank you for reading my book. If you enjoyed the book, please share your thoughts and post a review on the book retailer's website. It would be greatly appreciated!

Best wishes,
Catalina Morris